SHOP DRAWINGS
OF
SHAKER FURNITURE
AND
WOODENWARE

VOLUME I

MEASURED DRAWINGS
BY
EJNER HANDBERG

THE BERKSHIRE TRAVELLER PRESS
Stockbridge, Massachusetts

BOOKS OF SHAKER INTEREST BY EJNER HANDBERG
FROM BERKSHIRE TRAVELLER PRESS

Shop Drawings of Shaker Furniture and Woodenware,
Vol. I, Vol. II, Vol. III
Shop Drawings of Shaker Iron and Tinware
Measured Drawings of Shaker Furniture and Woodenware

ALSO BY EJNER HANDBERG:
Measured Drawings of Eighteenth-Century American Furniture

ISBN 0-912944-09-9
Library of Congress No. 73-83797

Printed in the United States of America by Studley Press, Dalton, MA 01226

FOREWORD

This is not an attempt to write a book about the Shakers and their furniture. There are already excellent books which serve that purpose. I refer especially to those by Dr. and Mrs. Edward Deming Andrews. Rather, this is a collection of measured drawings made to scale and with dimensions and details accurately copied from Shaker pieces which have been in my shop for restoration or reproduction. These drawings and patterns have been accumulated over a period of many years of interest in the woodwork of the New England and New York State Shakers.

Ejner P. Handberg

SHAKER REWARD OF MERIT

This Shaker reward of Merit was given to a young Shaker School boy of Hancock, Massachusetts during the nineteenth century. The drawings depict Shakers at work and play during two seasons.

It reads as follows:

The bearer Mr. Elijah Barker receives this as a token of the praise he merits. For his faithfulness and good behavier in schools from his teacher. S.A.P.

Reward of Merit
   In the Shaker Manner
To Ejner Handberg
From Faith Andrews
      Pittsfield, Mass. May 1, 1972

An expression of thanks for
your understanding and
appreciation of Shaker furniture.
   Collectors of this furniture are
indeed fortunate to know of your
work and have benefited by your
advice and help.
   When a restored piece leaves
your shop to take its place in
the "world" one is reminded
of the virtues of the early Be-
lievers. Honesty, simplicity and
humility were their guiding
principles. When these are
adapted by an artisan today
we approach perfection in
workmanship.
                        F. A.

CONTENTS

NOTES TO THE CRAFTSMAN OR COLLECTOR

White pine was the most common wood used for furniture like cupboards, chests of drawers, benches, woodboxes and many other items.

Bedposts, chairposts and all parts requiring strength were usually made of hard maple or yellow birch.

Maple, birch and cherry were used for legs on trestle tables, drop leaf tables and stands. The tops were often pine. Square legs are tapered on the inner surfaces only.

Sometimes candlestands, work stands and sewing stands were made entirely of cherry, maple or birch. The legs are dovetailed to the shaft and the grain should run as nearly parallel to the general direction of the leg as possible. A thin metal plate should be fastened to the underside of the shaft and extend about three quarters of an inch along the base of each leg with a screw or nail put in the leg to keep them from spreading.

Parts for chairs and stools were mostly hard maple with an occasional chair made of curly or bird's-eye maple. Birch, cherry and butternut were used less often.

Oval boxes and carriers were nearly always made of maple. The bottoms and covers were fitted with quarter-sawn, edge-grain pine which is less apt to cup or warp than flat-grained boards. First the "fingers" or "lappers" are cut on the maple bands, then they are steamed and wrapped around an oval form and the fingers fastened with small copper or iron rivets (tacks). After they are dry and sanded the pine disks are fitted into the bottom and cover and fastened with small square copper or iron brads.

In New York State and New England, the woods used for the many different small pieces of cabinet work and woodenware were white pine, maple, cherry, yellow birch, butternut and native walnut. They were often finished with a coat of thin paint, or stained and varnished, or sometimes left with a natural finish.

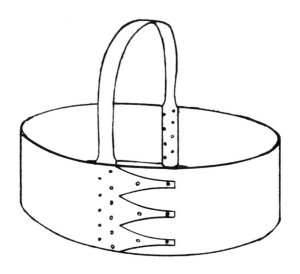

" THAT WHICH HAS IN ITSELF THE HIGHEST USE
POSSESSES THE GREATEST BEAUTY "

PINE CUPBOARD.

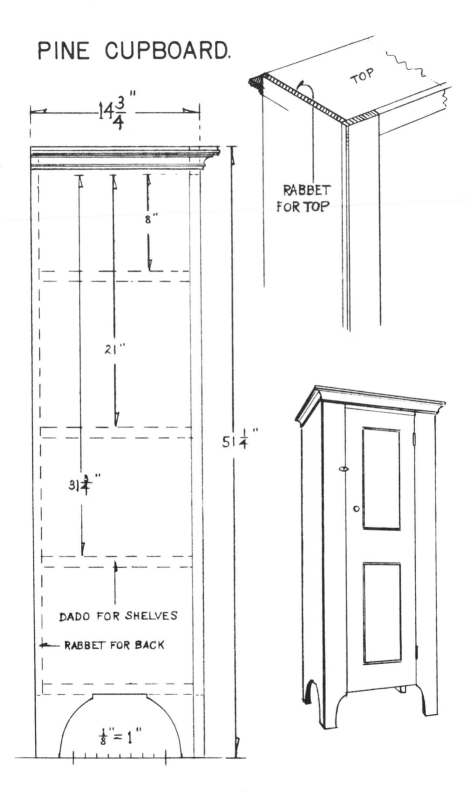

$14\frac{3}{4}$ "

8 "

21"

$51\frac{1}{4}$ "

$31\frac{3}{4}$ "

DADO FOR SHELVES

RABBET FOR BACK

$\frac{1}{8}$ " = 1 "

TOP

RABBET
FOR TOP

2

PINE CUPBOARD.

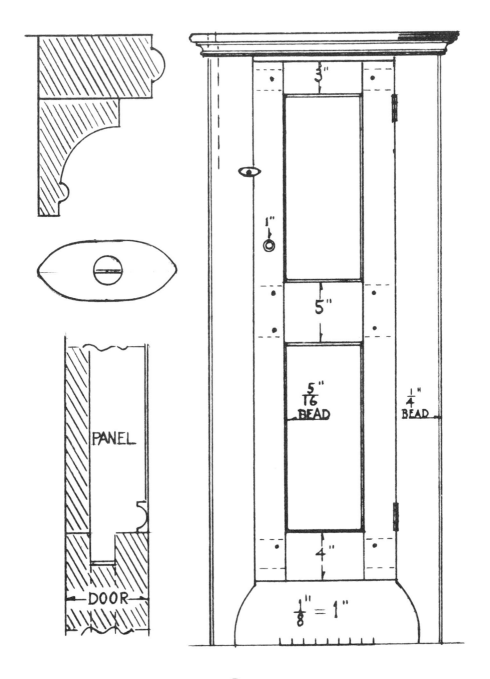

PANEL

DOOR

$\frac{3}{8}$"

1"

5"

$\frac{5}{16}$" BEAD

$\frac{1}{4}$" BEAD

4"

$\frac{1}{8}$" = 1"

3

BED
MAPLE AND WHITEWOOD

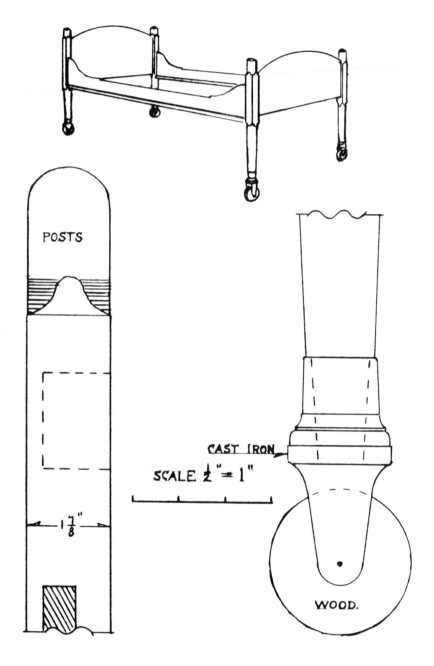

POSTS

CAST IRON

SCALE $\frac{1}{2}" = 1"$

$1\frac{7}{8}"$

WOOD.

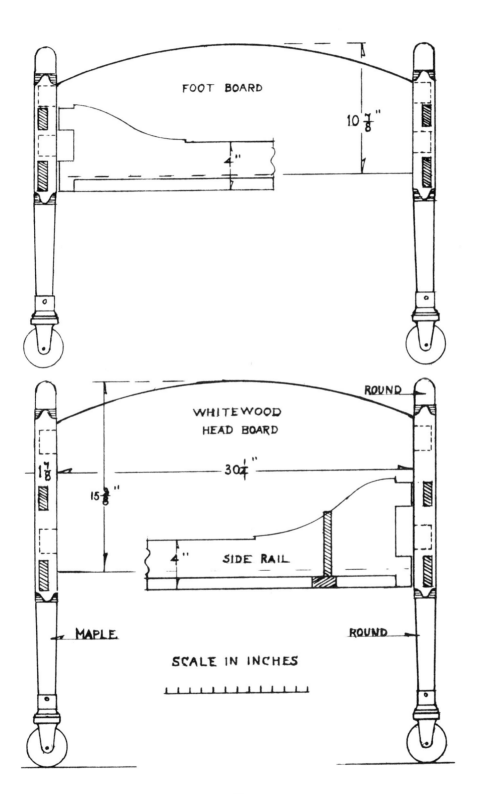

FOOT BOARD

$10\frac{7}{8}$ "

4"

WHITEWOOD
HEAD BOARD

ROUND

$1\frac{7}{8}$

$15\frac{7}{8}$ "

$30\frac{1}{4}$ "

4"   SIDE RAIL

MAPLE

ROUND

SCALE IN INCHES

5

SEWING DESK

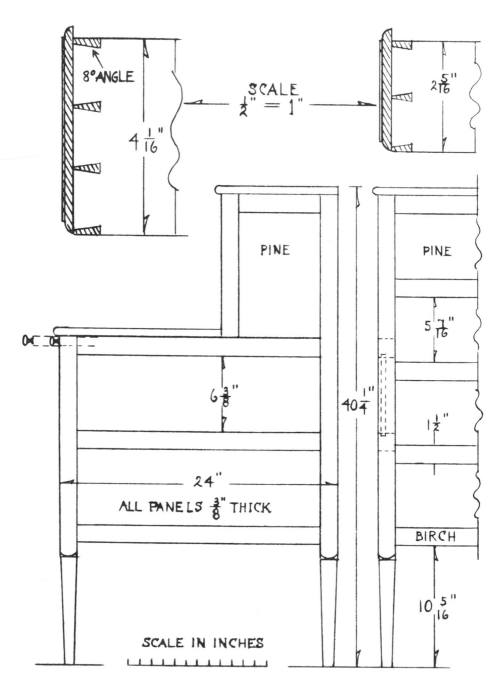

8°ANGLE

$4\frac{1}{16}$"

$2\frac{5}{16}$"

SCALE $\frac{1}{2}$" = 1"

PINE

PINE

$5\frac{7}{16}$"

$6\frac{3}{8}$"

$40\frac{1}{4}$"

$1\frac{1}{2}$"

24"

ALL PANELS $\frac{3}{8}$" THICK

BIRCH

$10\frac{5}{16}$"

SCALE IN INCHES

SEWING DESK

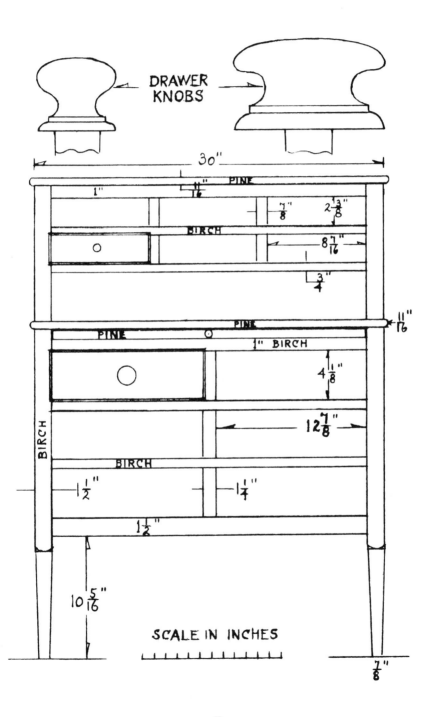

DRAWER KNOBS

30"

PINE

1"   1 1/16"

7/8"   2 3/8"

BIRCH

8 7/16"

3/4"

PINE   11/16"

PINE

1" BIRCH

4 1/8"

12 7/8"

BIRCH

1 1/2"   1 1/4"

1 1/2"

10 5/16"

SCALE IN INCHES

7/8"

7

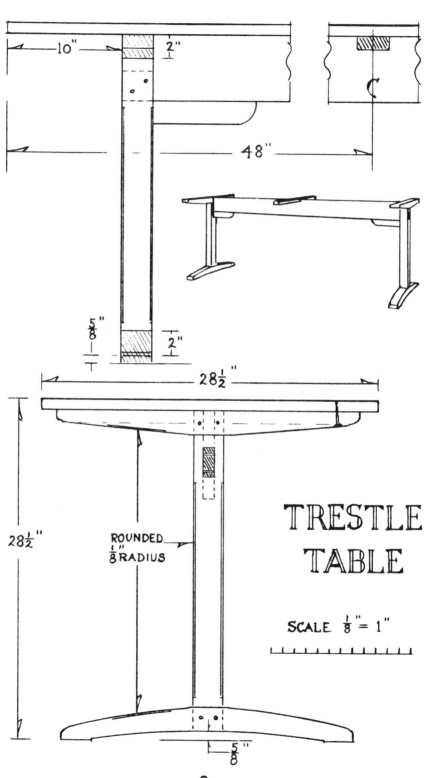

10"

2"

48"

C

$\frac{5}{8}$"

2"

$28\frac{1}{2}$"

$28\frac{1}{2}$"

ROUNDED
$\frac{1}{8}$" RADIUS

$\frac{5}{8}$"

TRESTLE
TABLE

SCALE $\frac{1}{8}$" = 1"

B

TRESTLE TABLE

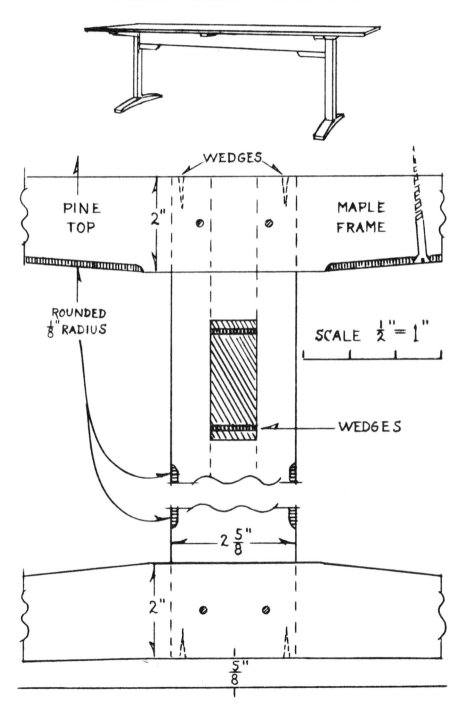

WEDGES

PINE
TOP

2"

MAPLE
FRAME

ROUNDED
$\frac{1}{8}$" RADIUS

SCALE $\frac{1}{2}$" = 1"

WEDGES

$2\frac{5}{8}$"

2"

$\frac{5}{8}$"

SEWING TABLE.

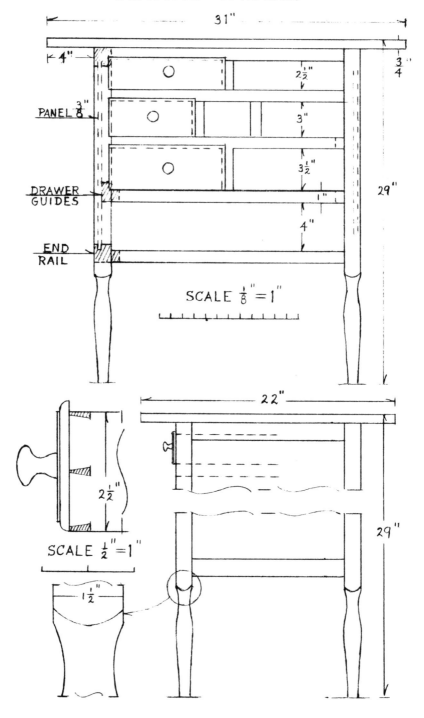

31"

4"

3/4"

2 1/2"

PANEL 3/8"

3"

3 1/2"

DRAWER
GUIDES

1"

END
RAIL

4"

29"

SCALE 1/8" = 1"

22"

2 1/2"

29"

SCALE 1/2" = 1"

1 1/2"

WORK TABLE.

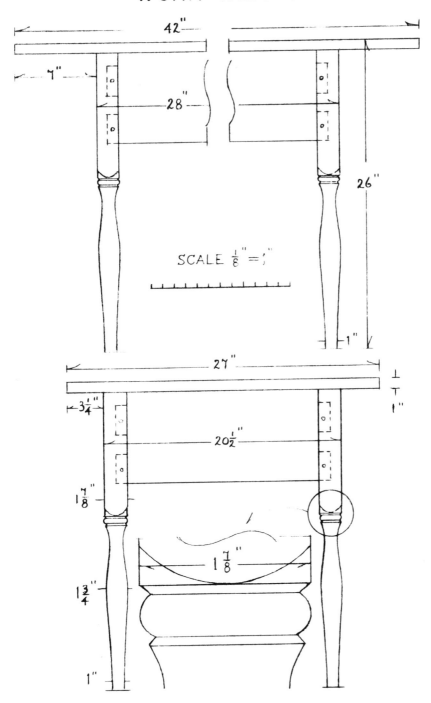

42"

7"

28"

26"

1"

SCALE ⅛" = 1"

27"

3¼"

20½"

1⅞"

1⅞"

1¾"

1"

1"

11

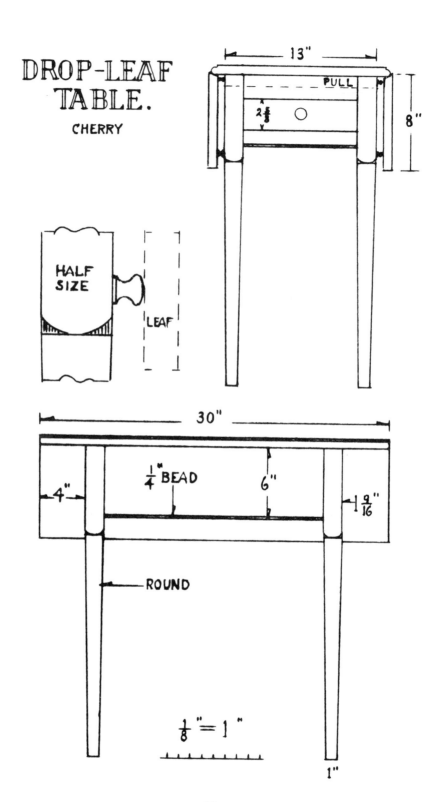

DROP-LEAF TABLE.

CHERRY

13"

PULL

2 5/8

8"

HALF SIZE

LEAF

30"

1/4" BEAD

6"

4"

1 9/16"

ROUND

1/8" = 1"

1"

DROP-LEAF
TABLE

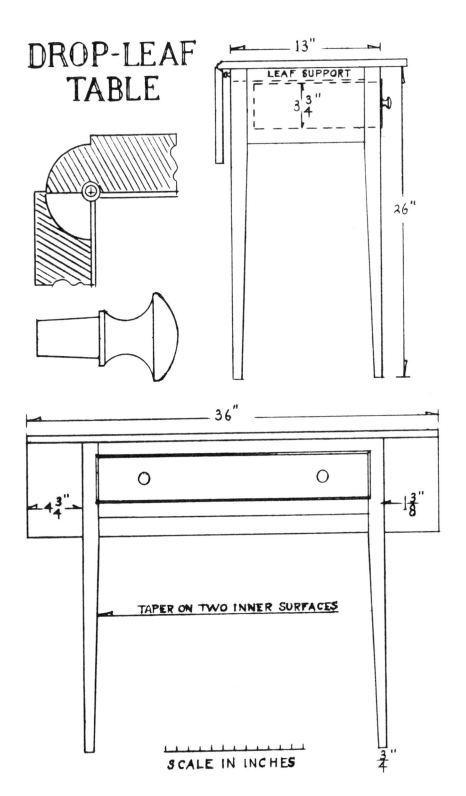

13"

LEAF SUPPORT

$3\frac{3}{4}$"

26"

36"

$4\frac{3}{4}$"

$1\frac{3}{8}$"

TAPER ON TWO INNER SURFACES

SCALE IN INCHES

$\frac{3}{4}$"

13

SEWING STAND.

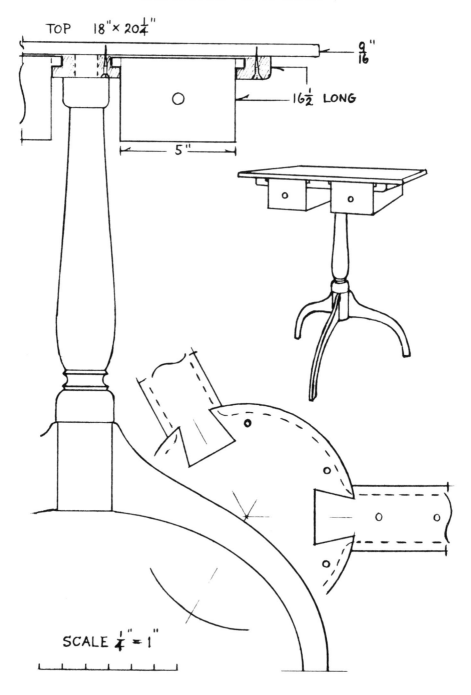

TOP   18" × 20¼"

$\frac{9}{16}$"

16½ LONG

5"

SCALE ¼" = 1"

WORKSTAND.

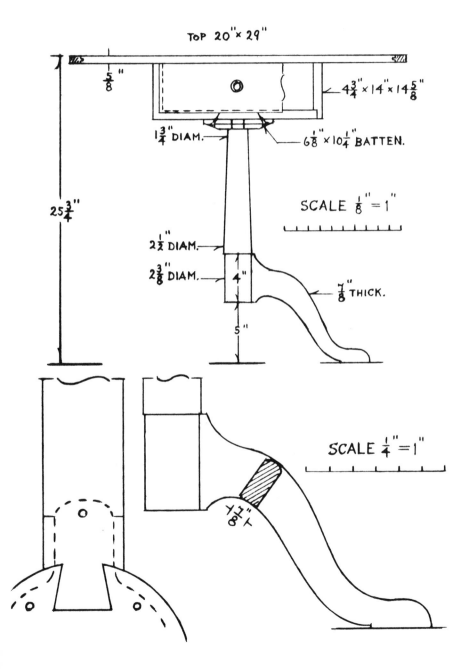

TOP 20" × 29"

$\frac{5}{8}$"

$4\frac{3}{4}$" × 14" × 14$\frac{5}{8}$"

$1\frac{3}{4}$" DIAM.

$6\frac{1}{8}$" × 10$\frac{1}{4}$" BATTEN.

$25\frac{3}{4}$"

SCALE $\frac{1}{8}$" = 1"

$2\frac{1}{2}$" DIAM.

$2\frac{3}{8}$" DIAM.

4"

$\frac{7}{8}$" THICK.

5"

SCALE $\frac{1}{4}$" = 1"

$\frac{7}{8}$"

15

PEG-LEG STAND.

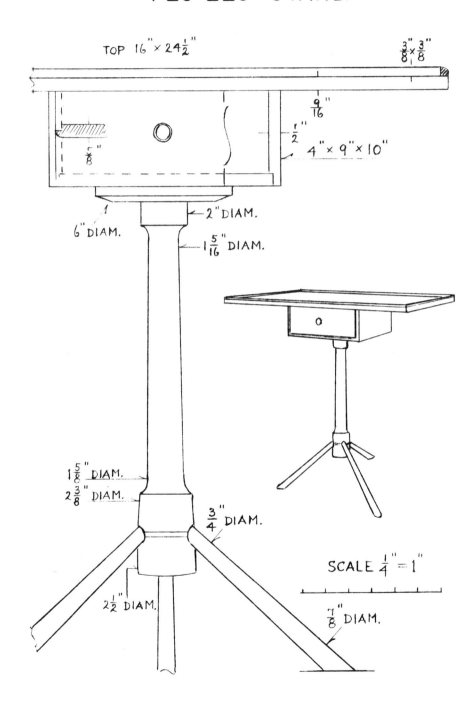

TOP 16" × 24½"

$\frac{3}{8}$" × $\frac{3}{8}$"

$\frac{9}{16}$"

$\frac{1}{2}$"

$\frac{5}{8}$"

4" × 9" × 10"

2" DIAM.

1$\frac{5}{16}$" DIAM.

6" DIAM.

1$\frac{5}{8}$" DIAM.

2$\frac{3}{8}$" DIAM.

$\frac{3}{4}$" DIAM.

2$\frac{1}{2}$" DIAM.

$\frac{7}{8}$" DIAM.

SCALE $\frac{1}{4}$" = 1"

CANDLESTAND.

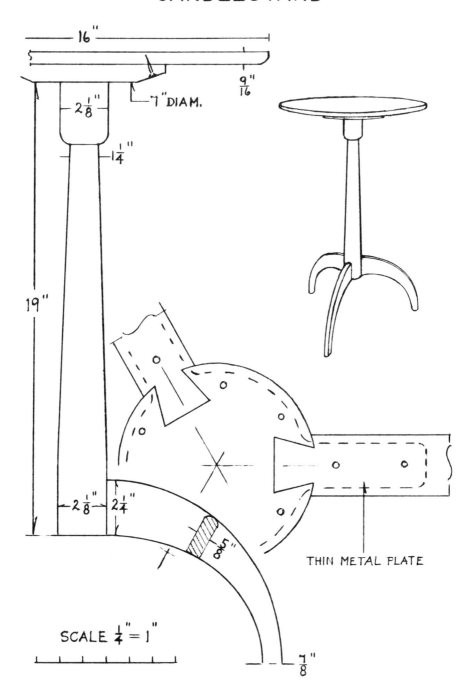

16"

$\frac{9}{16}$

7"DIAM.

$2\frac{1}{8}$"

$1\frac{1}{4}$"

19"

$2\frac{1}{8}$" → ← $2\frac{1}{4}$"

$\frac{5}{8}$"

THIN METAL PLATE

SCALE $\frac{1}{4}$" = 1"

$\frac{7}{8}$"

TOWEL RACK.

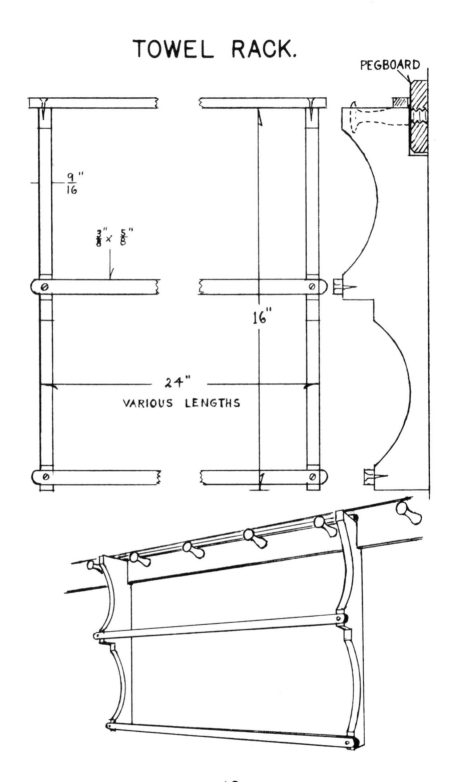

PEGBOARD

$\frac{9}{16}$"

$\frac{3}{8}$" × $\frac{5}{8}$"

16"

24"

VARIOUS LENGTHS

18

PINE TOWEL RACK

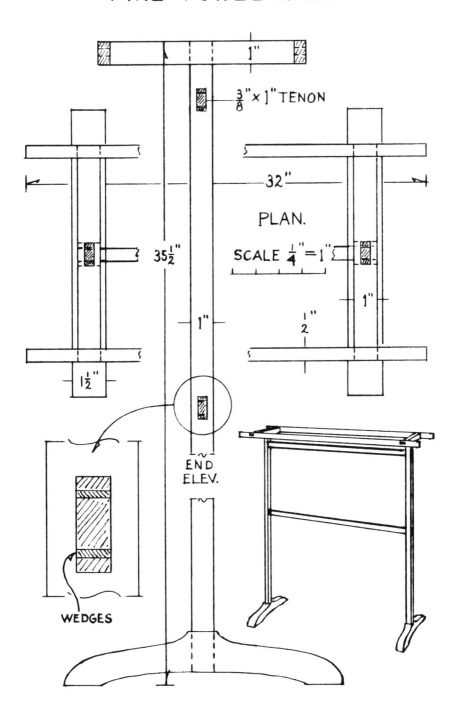

1"

$\frac{3}{8}$" x 1" TENON

32"

PLAN.

SCALE $\frac{1}{4}$" = 1"

35$\frac{1}{2}$"

1"

1"

$\frac{1}{2}$"

1$\frac{1}{2}$"

END
ELEV.

WEDGES

LOOKING GLASS.

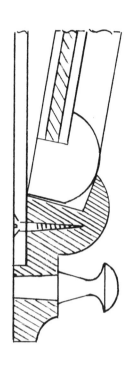

SCALE $\frac{3}{16}$" = 1"

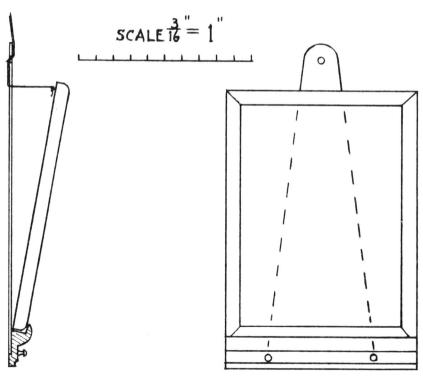

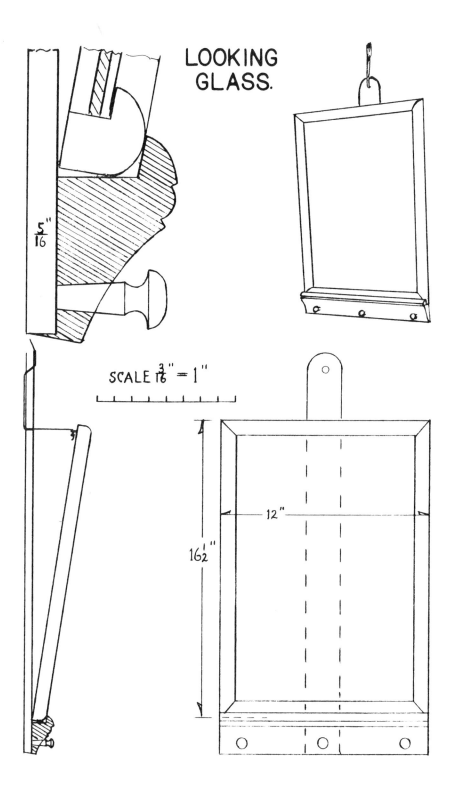

LOOKING
GLASS.

SCALE $\frac{3}{16}$" = 1"

$\frac{5}{16}$"

12"

$16\frac{1}{2}$"

$\frac{3}{8}$

TABLE -DESK.

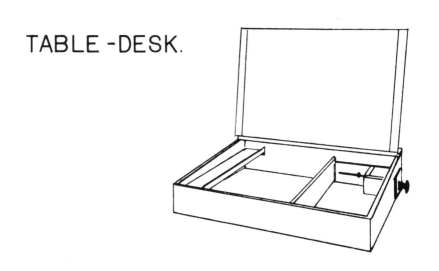

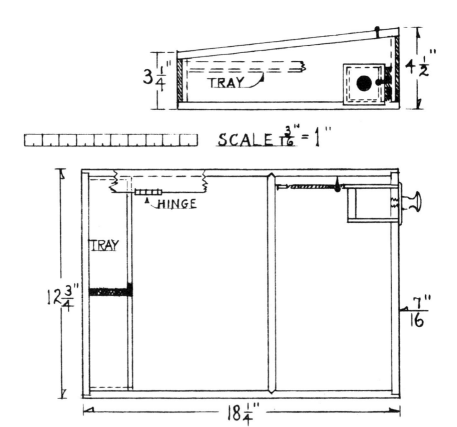

$3\frac{1}{4}$" TRAY $4\frac{1}{2}$"

SCALE $\frac{3}{16}$" = 1"

HINGE

TRAY

$12\frac{3}{4}$"

$\frac{7}{16}$"

$18\frac{1}{4}$"

22

TABLE-DESK.
CHERRY AND PINE

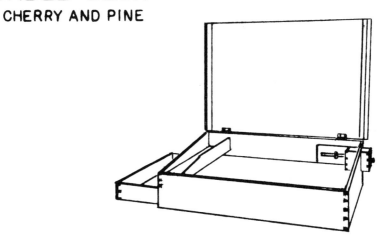

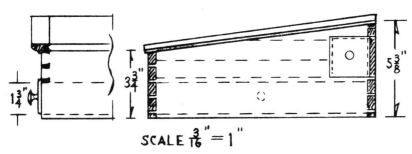

$1\frac{3}{4}"$

$3\frac{3}{4}"$

$5\frac{3}{8}"$

SCALE $\frac{3}{16}" = 1"$

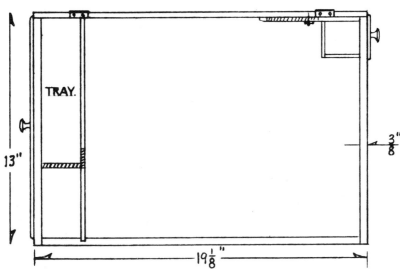

TRAY.

13"

$\frac{3}{8}"$

$19\frac{1}{8}"$

23

KNOBS AND PULLS.

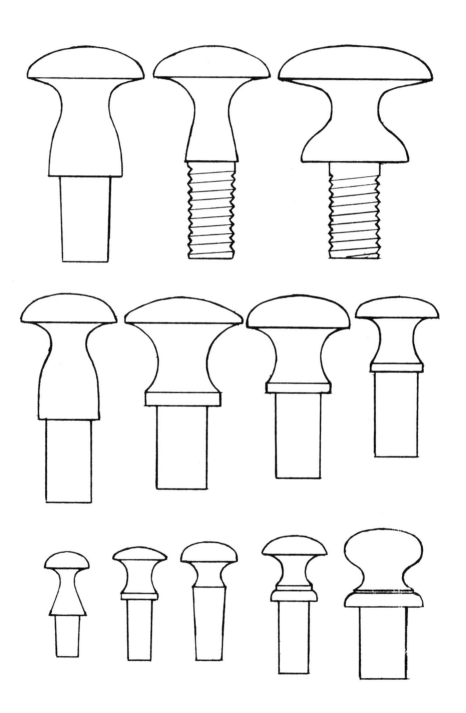

WALL-PEGS.

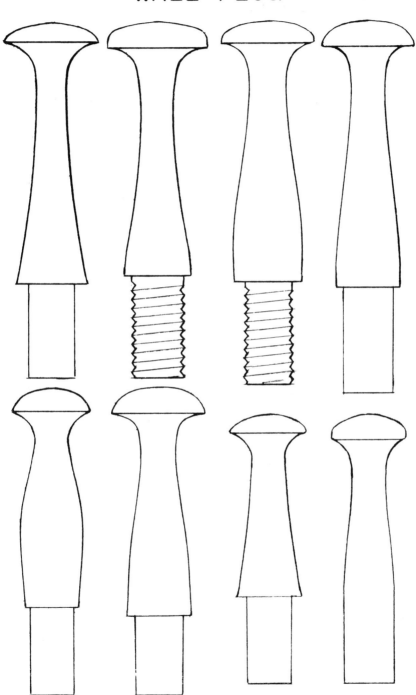

SMALL BENCH.

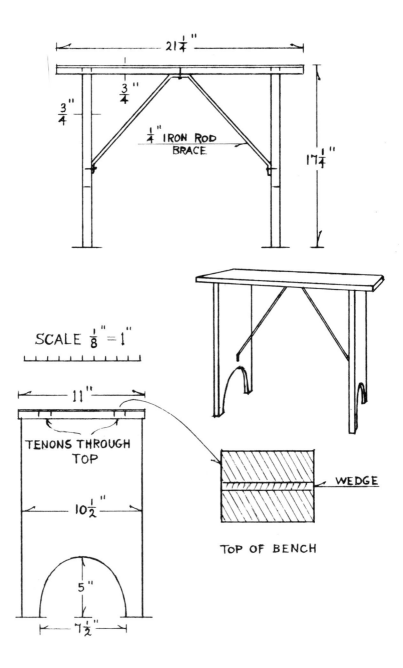

21¼"

¾"

¾"

¼" IRON ROD
BRACE

17¼"

SCALE ⅛" = 1"

11"

TENONS THROUGH
TOP

10½"

5"

7½"

WEDGE

TOP OF BENCH

PINE BENCH.

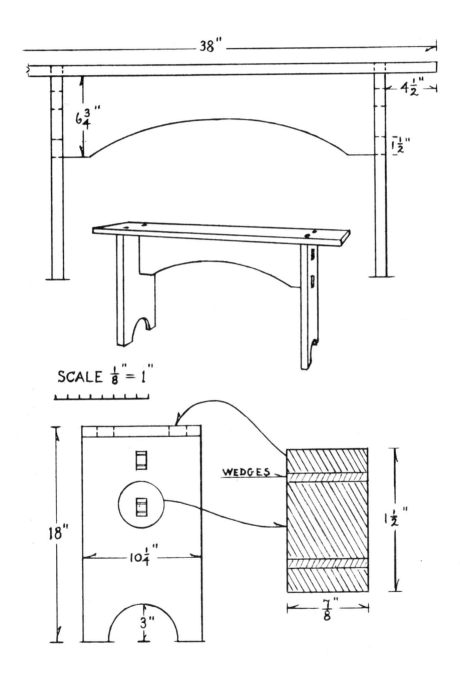

SCALE $\frac{1}{8}'' = 1''$

WEDGES

FOOT BENCHES.

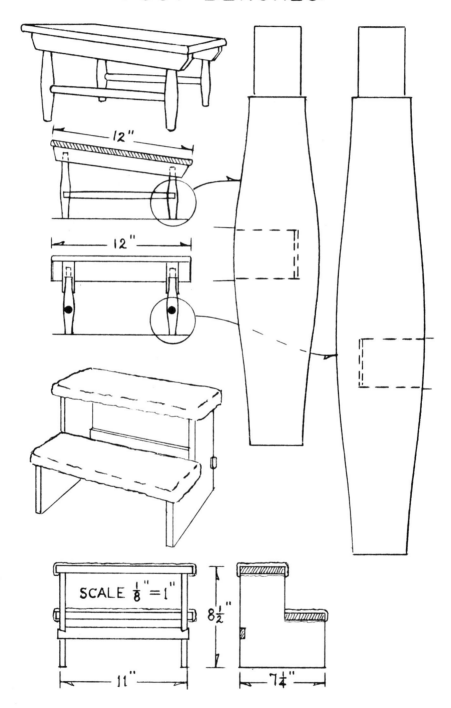

12"

12"

SCALE $\frac{1}{8}$" = 1"

8$\frac{1}{2}$"

11"

7$\frac{1}{4}$"

FOOTSTOOLS.

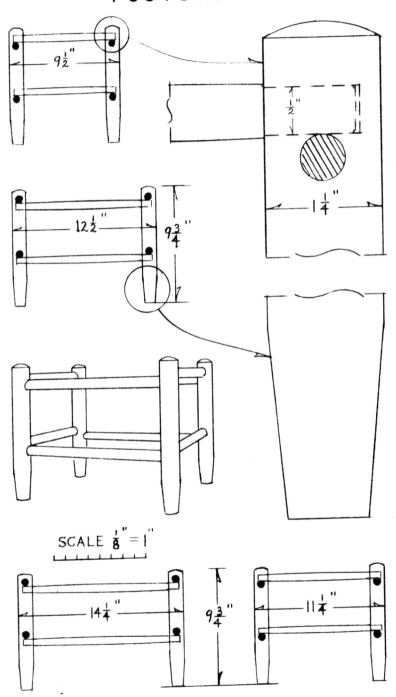

$9\frac{1}{2}$"

$1\frac{1}{2}$"

$1\frac{1}{4}$"

$12\frac{1}{2}$"

$9\frac{3}{4}$"

SCALE $\frac{1}{8}$" = 1"

$14\frac{1}{4}$"

$9\frac{3}{4}$"

$11\frac{1}{4}$"

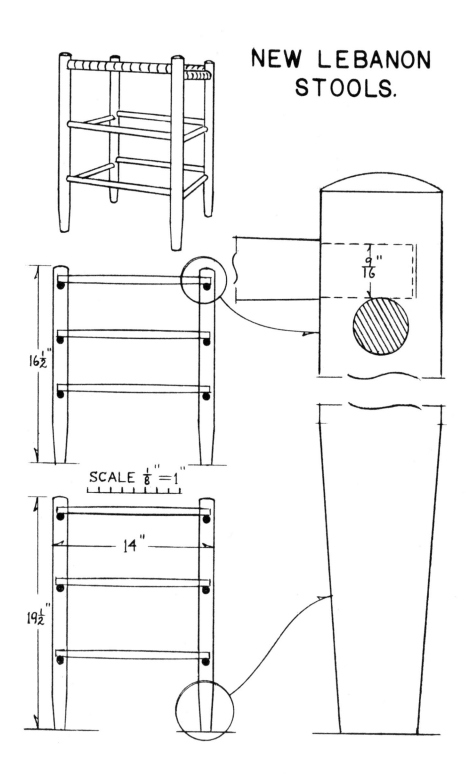

NEW LEBANON
STOOLS.

$\frac{9}{16}$"

$16\frac{1}{2}$"

SCALE $\frac{1}{8}$" = 1"

14"

$19\frac{1}{2}$"

30

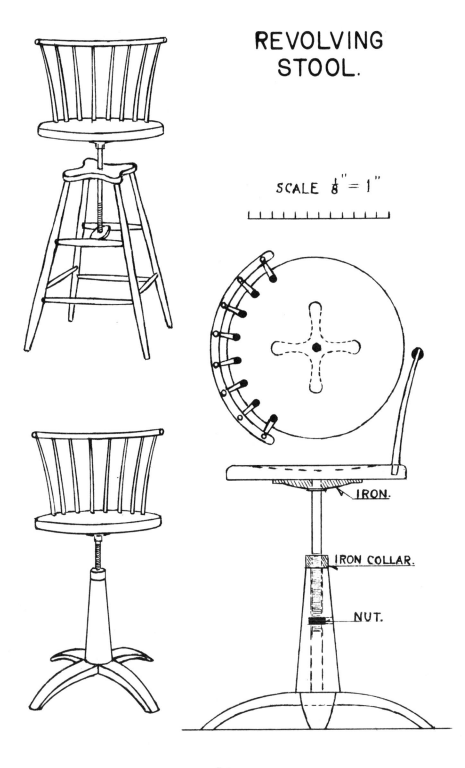

REVOLVING
STOOL.

SCALE $\frac{1}{8}" = 1"$

IRON.

IRON COLLAR.

NUT.

CHILD'S
BENT-WOOD
ROCKER.

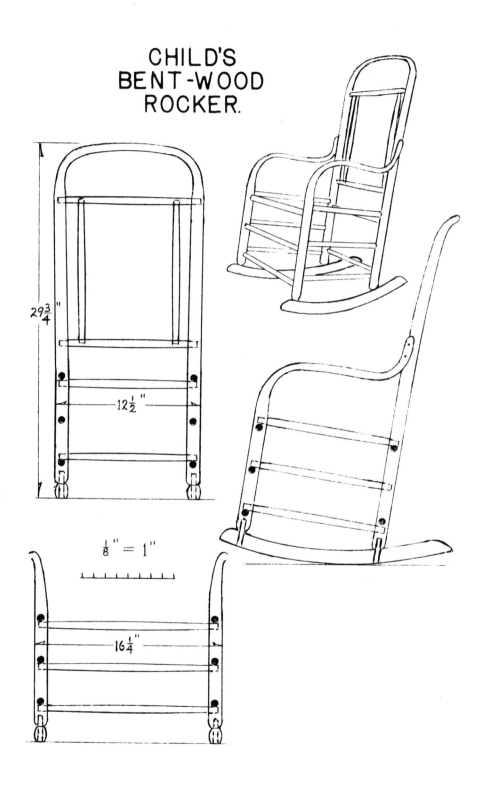

$29\frac{3}{4}''$

$12\frac{1}{2}''$

$\frac{1}{8}'' = 1''$

$16\frac{1}{4}''$

32

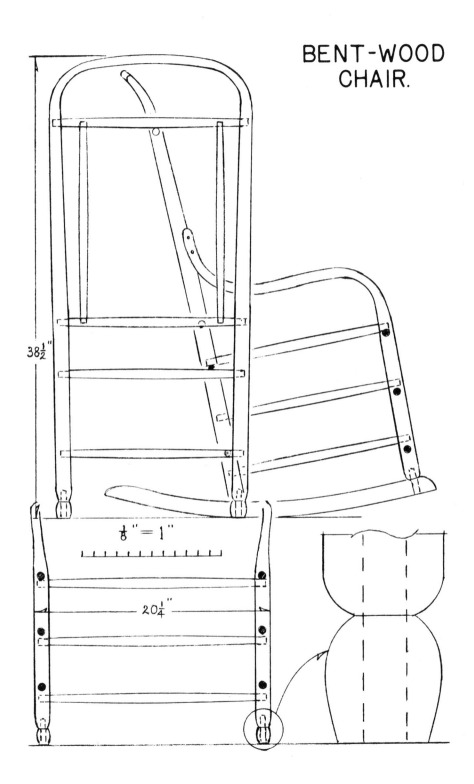

BENT-WOOD
CHAIR.

$38\frac{1}{2}$"

$\frac{1}{8}$" = 1"

$20\frac{1}{4}$"

33

CHILD'S CHAIR.

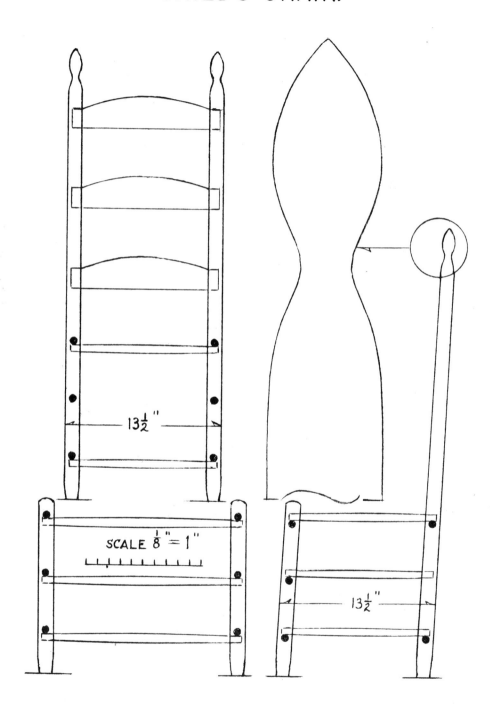

$13\frac{1}{2}$"

SCALE $\frac{1}{8}$" = 1"

$13\frac{1}{2}$"

CHILD'S CHAIR.

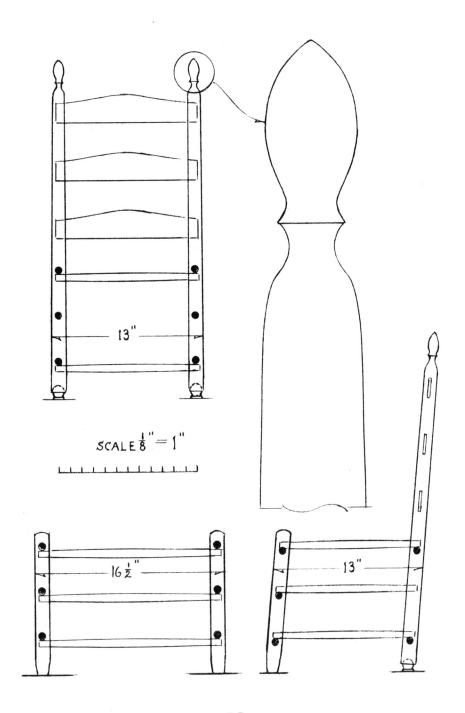

13"

SCALE $\frac{1}{8}$" = 1"

16$\frac{1}{2}$"

13"

35

TWO-SLAT
DINING CHAIR.

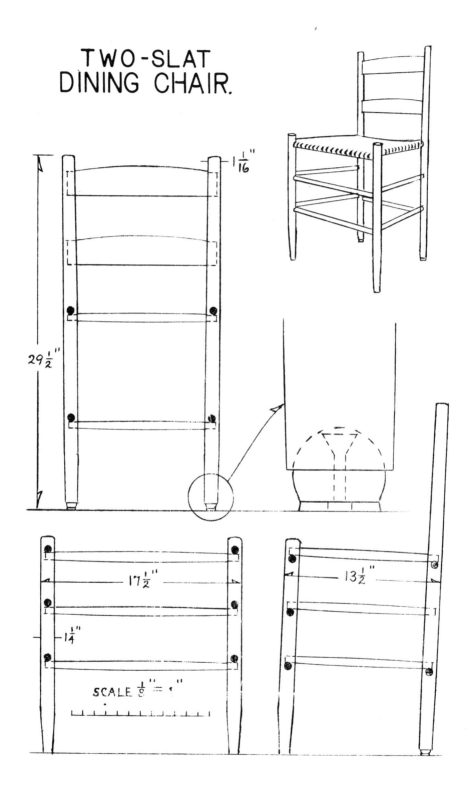

$1\frac{1}{16}''$

$29\frac{1}{2}''$

$17\frac{1}{2}''$

$1\frac{1}{4}''$

$13\frac{1}{2}''$

SCALE $\frac{1}{8}'' = 1''$

TWO-SLAT
DINING CHAIR

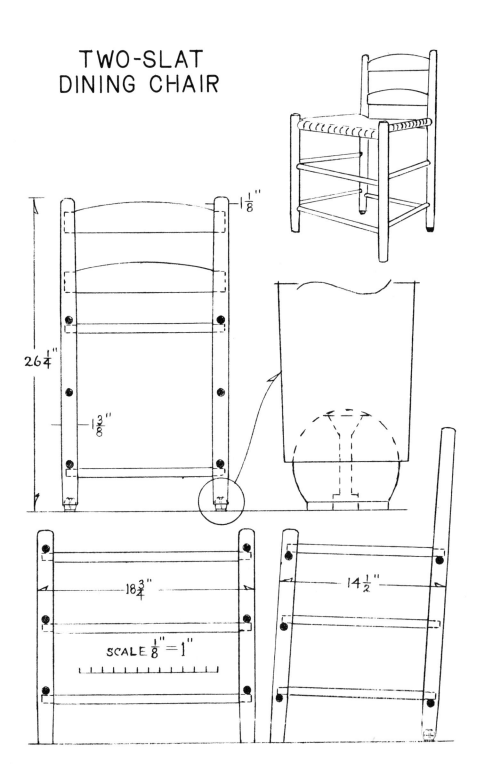

$1\frac{1}{8}''$

$26\frac{1}{4}''$

$1\frac{3}{8}''$

$18\frac{3}{4}''$

SCALE $\frac{1}{8}''=1''$

$14\frac{1}{2}''$

EARLY ROCKING CHAIR.

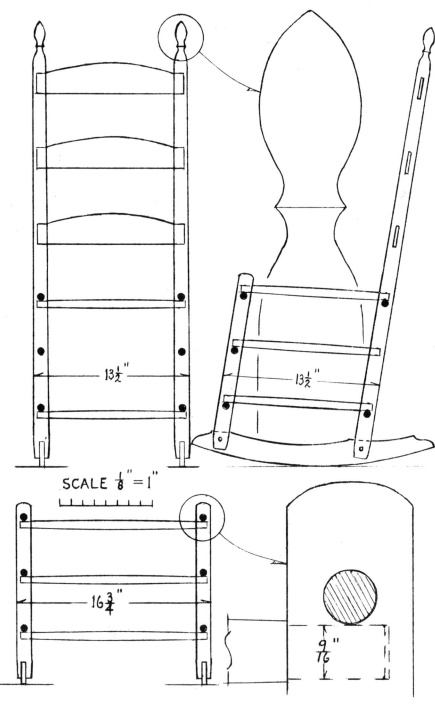

$13\frac{1}{2}''$

$13\frac{1}{2}''$

SCALE $\frac{1}{8}'' = 1''$

$16\frac{3}{4}''$

$\frac{9}{16}''$

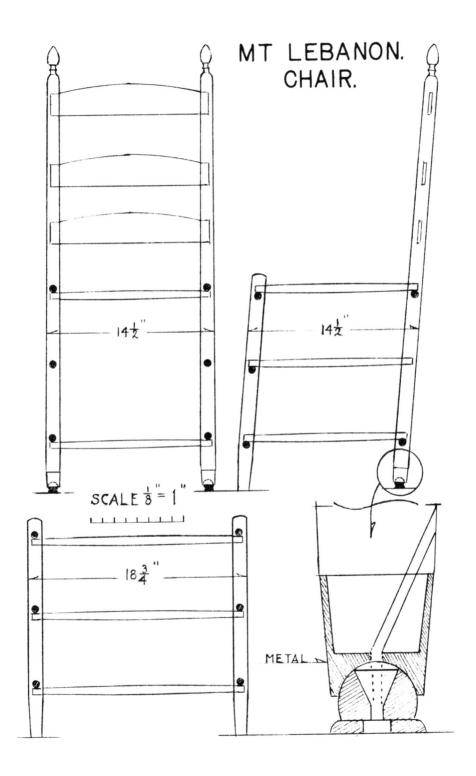

MT LEBANON.
CHAIR.

$14\frac{1}{2}$"

$14\frac{1}{2}$"

SCALE $\frac{1}{8}$" = 1"

$18\frac{3}{4}$"

METAL

MT. LEBANON
ARMCHAIR.

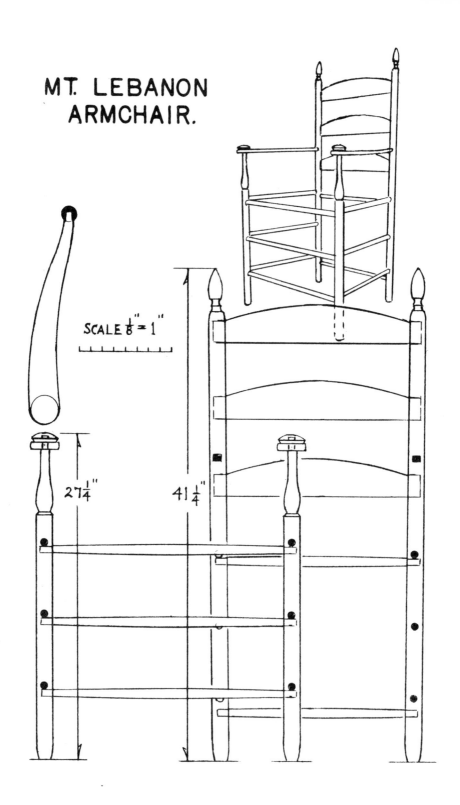

SCALE $\frac{1}{8}$" = 1"

$27\frac{1}{4}$"

$41\frac{1}{4}$"

MT. LEBANON ARMCHAIR.

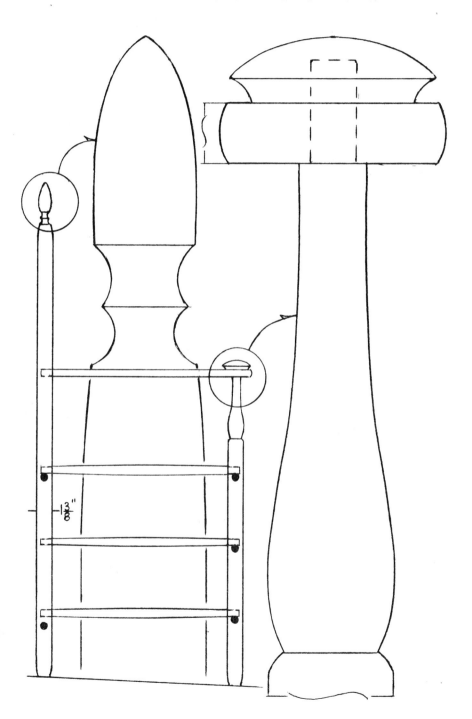

$1\frac{3}{8}"$

MT. LEBANON CHAIRS.

The following quotations and the descriptions
on the Plates are taken from a Shaker chair catalog
dated 1876.

" . . . a description and a representation of the
different sizes of chairs and foot benches which we
manufacture and sell. We would also call attention
of the public to the fact that there is no other
chair manufactory which is owned and operated by the
Shakers, except the one which is now in operation
and owned and operated by the Society of Shakers, at
Mount Lebanon, Columbia, county, N. Y. We deem it a
duty we owe the public to enlighten them in this
matter, owing to the fact that there are now several
manufacturers of chairs who have made and introduced
into market an imitation of our own styles of chairs,
which they sell for Shakers' Chairs, and which are
unquestionably bought by the public generally under
the impression that they are the real genuine article,
made by the Shakers at their establishment in Mount
Lebanon, N. Y. Of all the imitations of our chairs
which have come under our observation, there is none
which we would be willing to accept as our workmanship, nor would we be willing to stake our reputation
on their merits.

"The increasing demand for our chairs has prompted
us to increase the facilities for producing and
improving them. We have spared no expense or labor
in our endeavors to produce an article that cannot
be surpassed in any respect, and which combines all
the advantages of durability, simplicity and light-
ness.

"The bars across the top of back posts are intend-
ed for cushions, but will be furnished to order without additional cost.

"Many of our friends who see the Shakers' chairs for the first time may be led to suppose that the chair business is a new thing for the Shakers to engage in. This is not the fact, however, and may surprise even some of the oldest manufacturers to learn that the Shakers were pioneers in the business after the establishment of the independence of the country.

"The principles as well as the rules of the Society forbid the trustees or any of their assistants doing business on the credit system, either in the purchase or sale of merchandise, or making bargains or contracts. This we consider good policy, and a safe way of doing business, checking speculative or dishonest propensities, and averting financial panics and disasters. We sell with the understanding that all bills are to be cash.

"Look for our trade-mark before purchasing - no chair is genuine without it. Our trade-mark is a gold transfer, and is designed to be ornamental; but, if objectionable to purchasers, it can be easily removed without defacing the furniture in the least, by wetting a sponge or piece of cotton cloth with AQUA AMMONIA, and rubbing it until it is loosened."

The Shakers' Slat Back Chairs, with Rockers.

WORSTED LACE SEATS.

Showing a Comparison of Sizes.

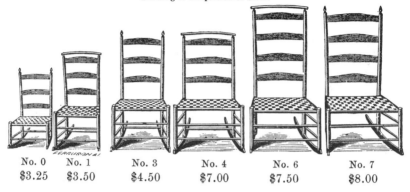

No. 0	No. 1	No. 3	No. 4	No. 6	No. 7
$3.25	$3.50	$4.50	$7.00	$7.50	$8.00

The Shakers' Web Back Chairs, With Rockers.

WORSTED LACE SEATS AND BACKS.

Showing a Comparison of Sizes.

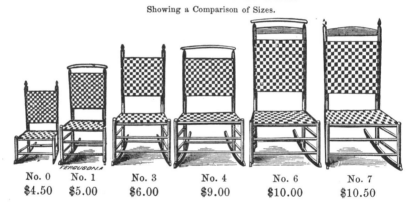

No. 0	No. 1	No. 3	No. 4	No. 6	No. 7
$4.50	$5.00	$6.00	$9.00	$10.00	$10.50

THE SHAKERS' UPHOLSTERED CHAIRS.

WITHOUT ARMS.

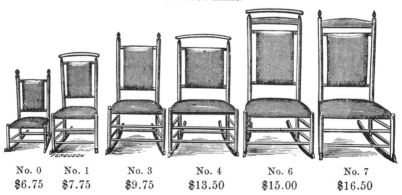

No. 0	No. 1	No. 3	No. 4	No. 6	No. 7
$6.75	$7.75	$9.75	$13.50	$15.00	$16.50

44

The Shakers' Slat Back Chairs, with Arms and Rockers.

WORSTED LACE SEATS.

Showing a Comparison of Sizes.

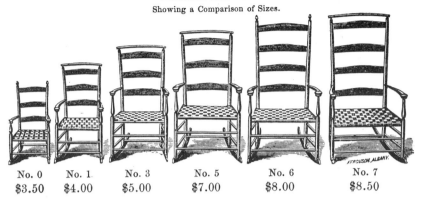

No. 0	No. 1	No. 3	No. 5	No. 6	No. 7
$3.50	$4.00	$5.00	$7.00	$8.00	$8.50

The Shakers' Web Back Chairs, with Arms and Rockers.

WORSTED LACE SEATS AND BACKS.

Showing a Comparison of Sizes.

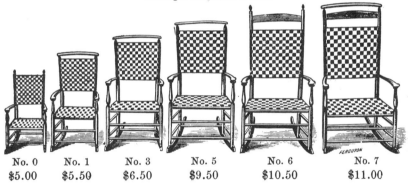

No. 0	No. 1	No. 3	No. 5	No. 6	No. 7
$5.00	$5.50	$6.50	$9.50	$10.50	$11.00

THE SHAKERS' UPHOLSTERED CHAIRS.

WITH ARMS AND ROCKERS.

No. 0	No. 1	No. 3	No. 5	No. 6	No. 7
$7.00	$8.25	$10.25	$13.50	$15.50	$17.00

45

MT. LEBANON CHAIR NO. 7.

"This is our largest chair, and on the top of the back posts is a bar which we attach to all the chairs which are designed for cushions.

"We have this chair with or without rockers or arms.

"Remember that all chairs are imitations which are not made and sold by the Society of Shakers, Mount Lebanon, N. Y. Don't let any outside party sell you the imitation or spurious chairs which may bear the name of Shaker chair."

$\frac{5}{8}$ "

$\frac{1"}{8} = 1"$

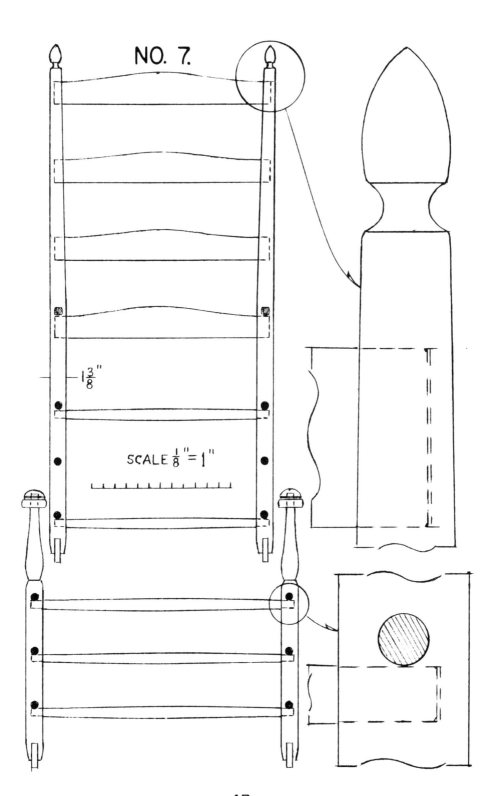

NO. 7.

$1\frac{3}{8}$"

SCALE $\frac{1}{8}$" = 1"

MT. LEBANON CHAIR NO. 6.

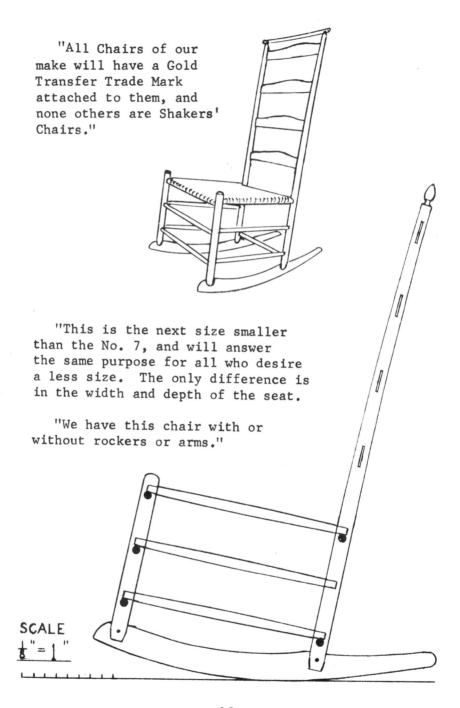

"All Chairs of our make will have a Gold Transfer Trade Mark attached to them, and none others are Shakers' Chairs."

"This is the next size smaller than the No. 7, and will answer the same purpose for all who desire a less size. The only difference is in the width and depth of the seat.

"We have this chair with or without rockers or arms."

SCALE
$\frac{1}{8}$" = 1"

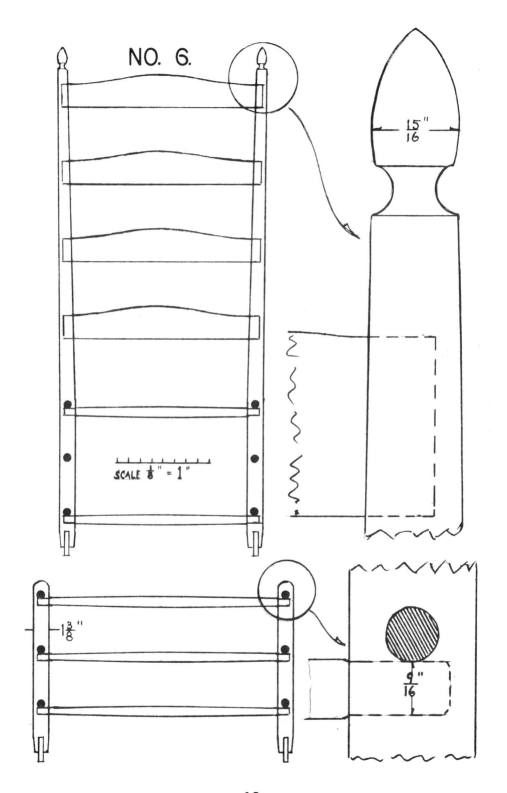

NO. 6.

SCALE $\frac{1}{8}$" = 1"

$\frac{15}{16}$"

$1\frac{3}{8}$"

$\frac{9}{16}$"

49

MT. LEBANON CHAIR NO. 5.

"This size is well adapted for
dining or office use, when an arm
chair is desirable. We have a
smaller size, with only two back
slats and plain top posts, for table
use, and without arms.

"We do not have this chair without the arms.

"The Shakers do not make or sell
any of the cheap quality of chairs,
but we claim for every one of them
the same quality and price invariably."

$\frac{1}{8}" = 1"$

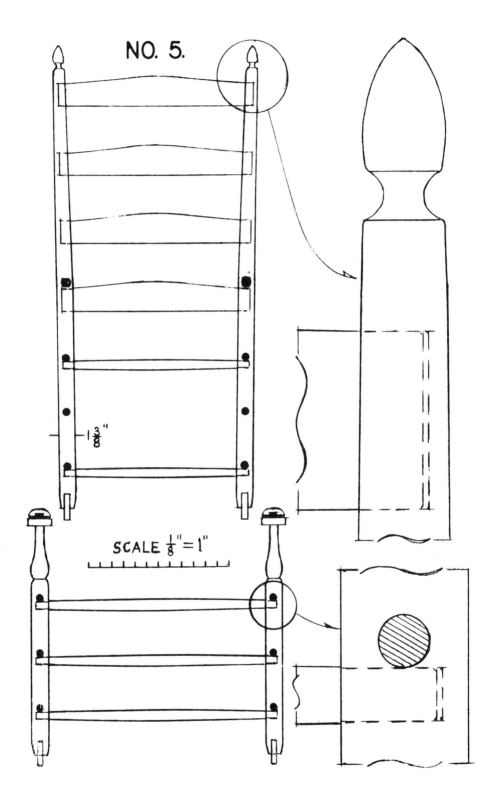

NO. 5.

$1\frac{3}{8}$"

SCALE $\frac{1}{8}$" = 1"

51

MT. LEBANON CHAIR NO. 4.

"This chair is a great favorite
with the ladies. It is broad on
the seat, and very easy. We do
not make this size with arms, and
the back is lower than the large
arm chairs, but have them with or
without rockers."

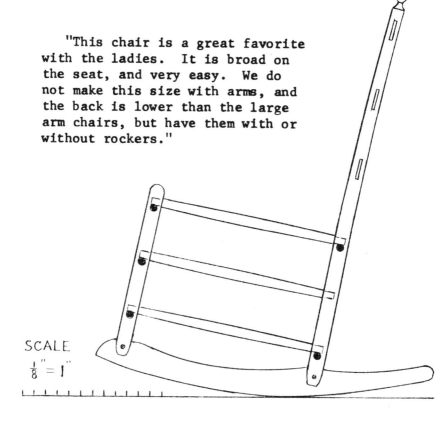

SCALE
$\frac{1}{8}'' = 1''$

MT. LEBANON CHAIR NO. 4.

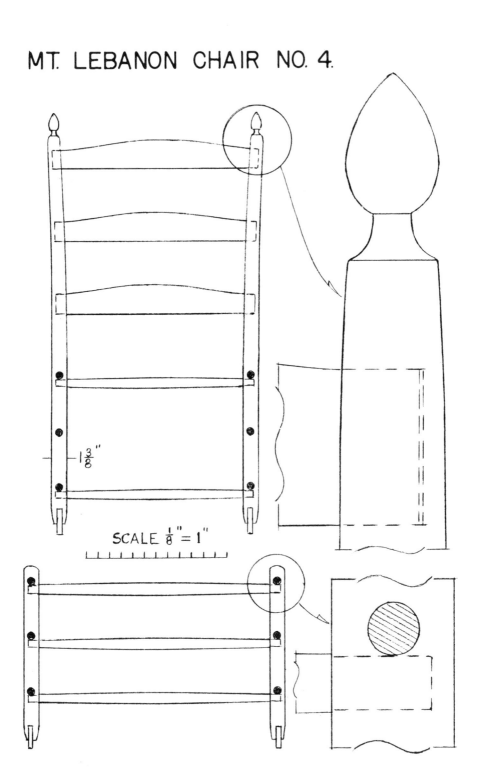

$1\frac{3}{8}''$

SCALE $\frac{1}{8}'' = 1''$

MT. LEBANON CHAIR NO. 3.

"This is a favorite
sewing chair, and for all
general purposes about
the chamber and sitting
room. We have this size
with arms, rockers, or
without either."

"Those who want a very comfortable
chair, and do not want to expend enough
for a cushioned chair, would do well
to get one with a web back. It is both
comfortable and neat, and requires only
a trifling additional cost more than
the slat backs."

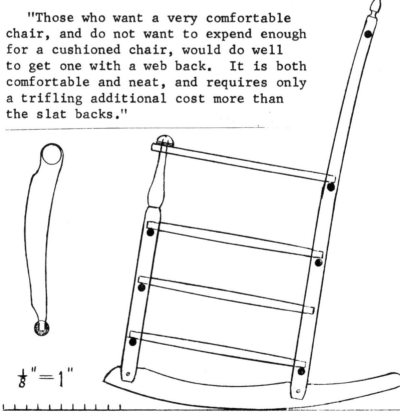

$\frac{1}{8}" = 1"$

MT. LEBANON CHAIR NO. 3.

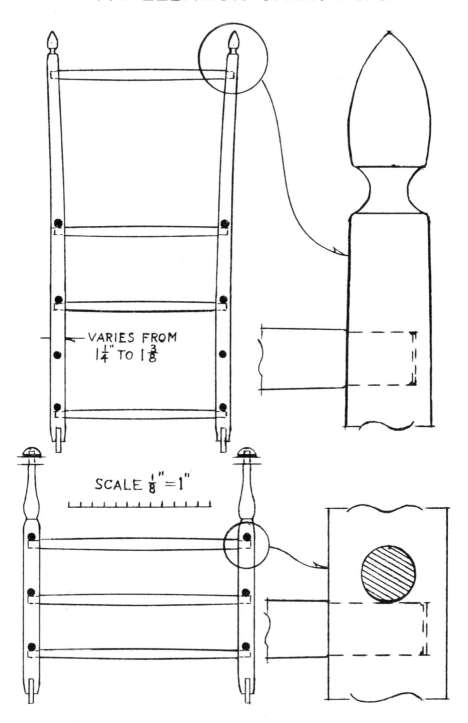

VARIES FROM $1\frac{1}{4}"$ TO $1\frac{3}{8}$

SCALE $\frac{1}{8}" = 1"$

MT. LEBANON CHAIR NO. I.

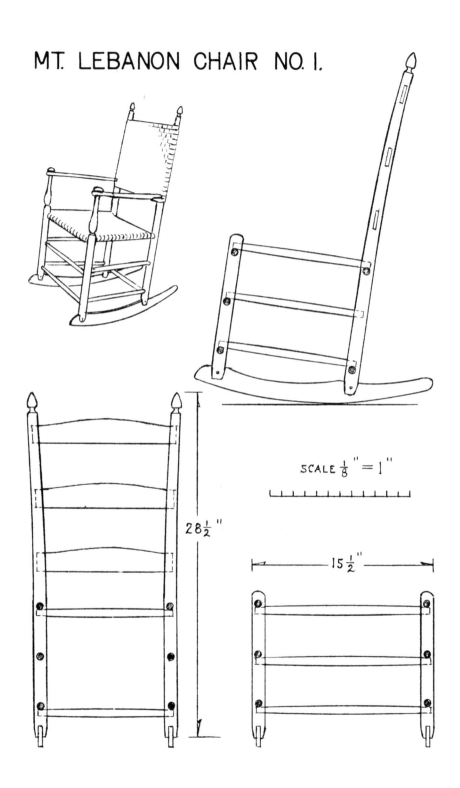

SCALE $\frac{1}{8}'' = 1''$

$28\frac{1}{2}''$

$15\frac{1}{2}''$

MT. LEBANON CHAIR NO. I.

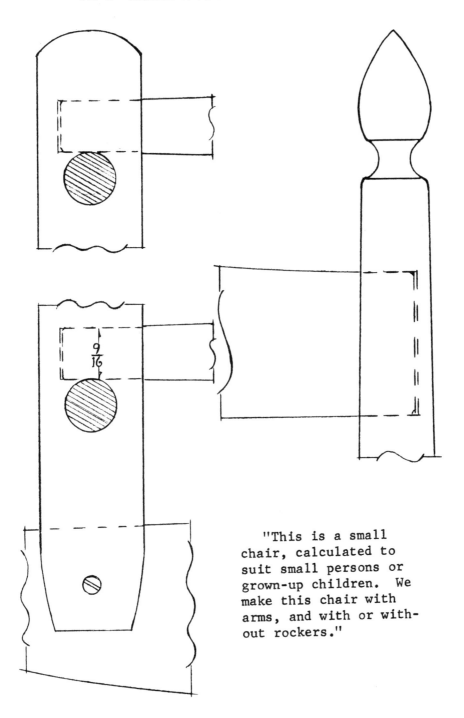

$\frac{9}{16}$

"This is a small
chair, calculated to
suit small persons or
grown-up children. We
make this chair with
arms, and with or with-
out rockers."

MT. LEBANON CHAIR NO. O.

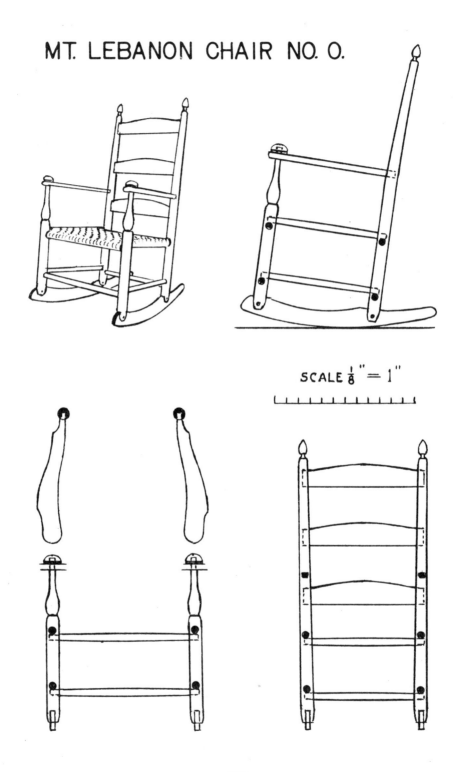

SCALE $\frac{1}{8}$" = 1"

MT. LEBANON CHAIR NO. O.

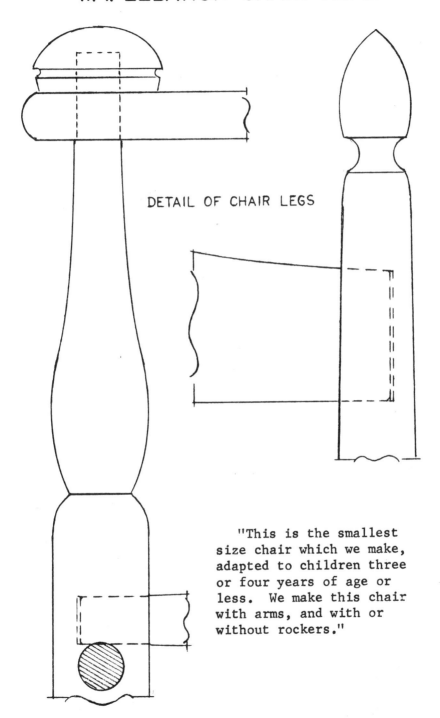

DETAIL OF CHAIR LEGS

"This is the smallest size chair which we make, adapted to children three or four years of age or less. We make this chair with arms, and with or without rockers."

CHAIR FINIALS.

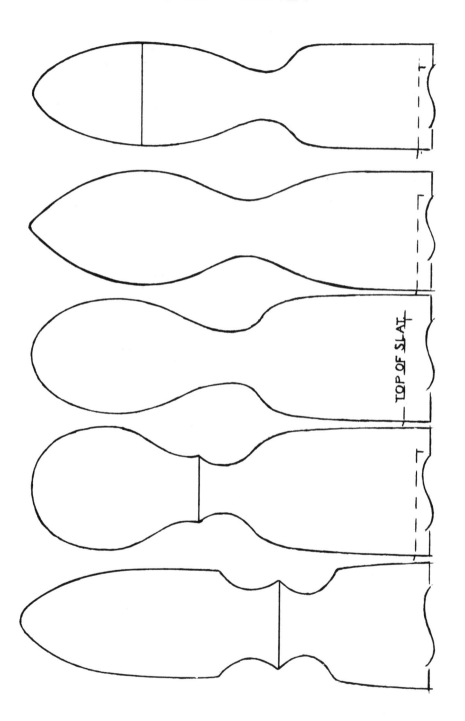

TOP OF SLAT

CHAIR FINIALS.

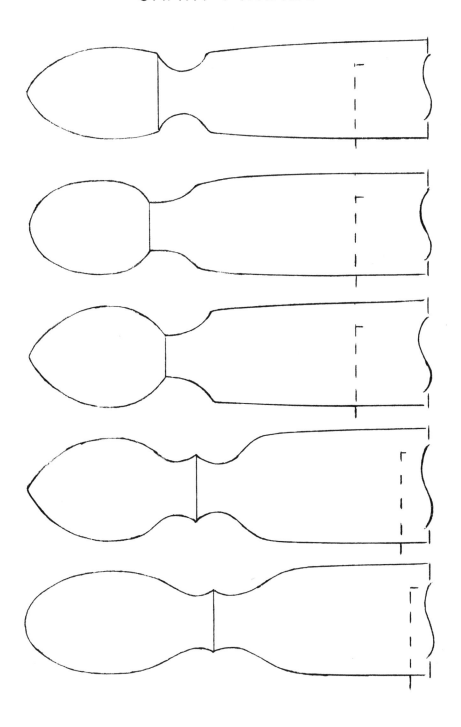

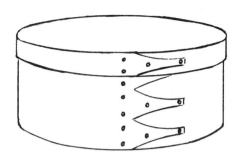

OVAL BOX.

INSIDE MEAS.
OF BOX $7\frac{1}{2}'' \times 10\frac{7}{8}''$

COVER TO FIT

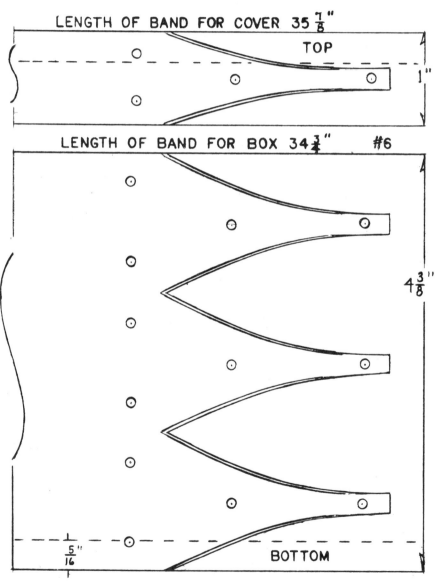

LENGTH OF BAND FOR COVER $35\frac{7}{8}''$

TOP

$1''$

LENGTH OF BAND FOR BOX $34\frac{3}{4}''$ #6

$4\frac{3}{8}''$

$\frac{5}{16}''$

BOTTOM

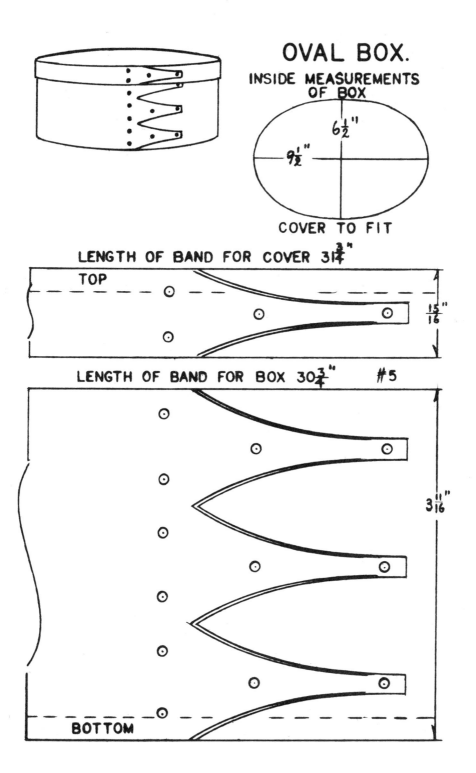

OVAL BOX.

INSIDE MEASUREMENTS OF BOX

$6\frac{1}{2}$"

$9\frac{1}{2}$"

COVER TO FIT

LENGTH OF BAND FOR COVER $31\frac{3}{4}$"

TOP

$\frac{15}{16}$"

LENGTH OF BAND FOR BOX $30\frac{3}{4}$"   #5

$3\frac{11}{16}$"

BOTTOM

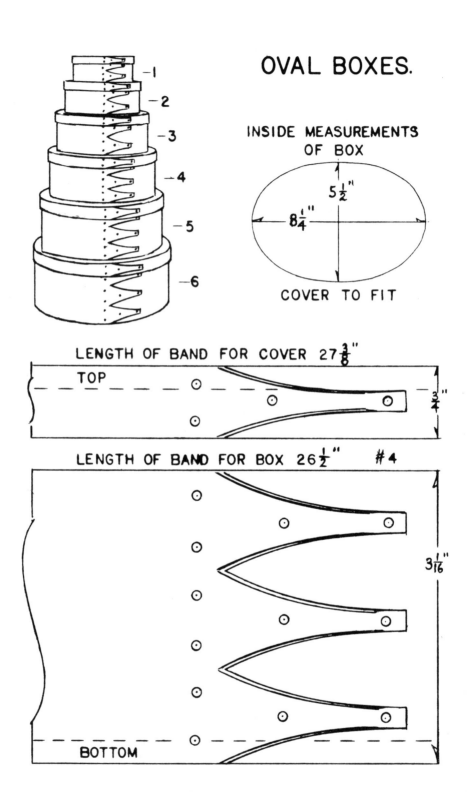

OVAL BOXES.

INSIDE MEASUREMENTS
OF BOX

$5\frac{1}{2}$"

$8\frac{1}{4}$"

COVER TO FIT

LENGTH OF BAND FOR COVER $27\frac{3}{8}$"

TOP

$\frac{3}{4}$"

LENGTH OF BAND FOR BOX $26\frac{1}{2}$"   #4

$3\frac{1}{16}$"

BOTTOM

64

OVAL BOXES.

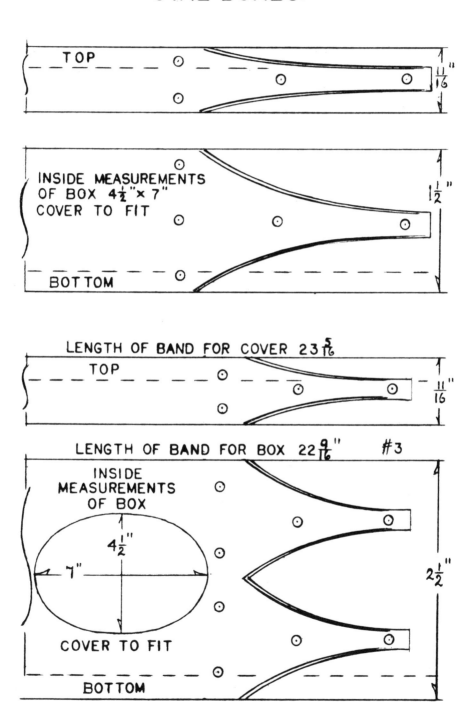

TOP

$\frac{11}{16}$"

INSIDE MEASUREMENTS
OF BOX 4½"× 7"
COVER TO FIT

1½"

BOTTOM

LENGTH OF BAND FOR COVER 23 $\frac{5}{16}$

TOP

$\frac{11}{16}$"

LENGTH OF BAND FOR BOX 22 $\frac{9}{16}$"   #3

INSIDE
MEASUREMENTS
OF BOX

4½"

7"

COVER TO FIT

2½"

BOTTOM

OVAL BOXES.

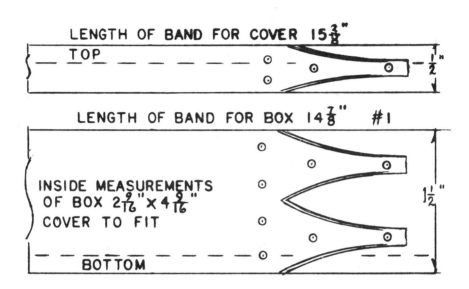

LENGTH OF BAND FOR COVER 15⅜"

TOP

½"

LENGTH OF BAND FOR BOX 14⅞"   #1

INSIDE MEASUREMENTS
OF BOX 2 9/16" X 4 9/16"
COVER TO FIT

1½"

BOTTOM

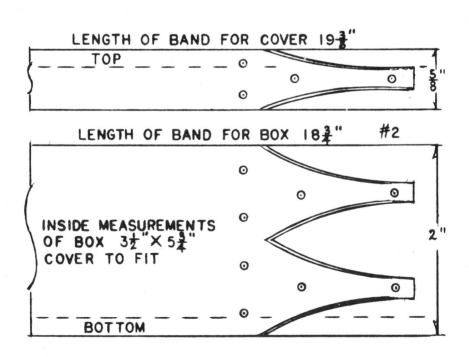

LENGTH OF BAND FOR COVER 19⅜"

TOP

⅝"

LENGTH OF BAND FOR BOX 18¾"   #2

INSIDE MEASUREMENTS
OF BOX 3½" X 5¾"
COVER TO FIT

2"

BOTTOM

SEWING BOX.

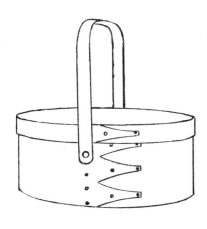

INSIDE MEASUREMENTS OF BOX

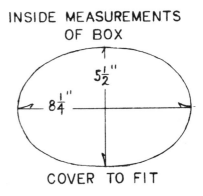

$5\frac{1}{2}''$

$8\frac{1}{4}''$

COVER TO FIT

LENGTH OF BAND FOR COVER $27\frac{3}{8}''$

TOP

$\frac{3}{4}''$

LENGTH OF BAND FOR BOX $26\frac{1}{2}''$

$3\frac{1}{16}''$

BOTTOM

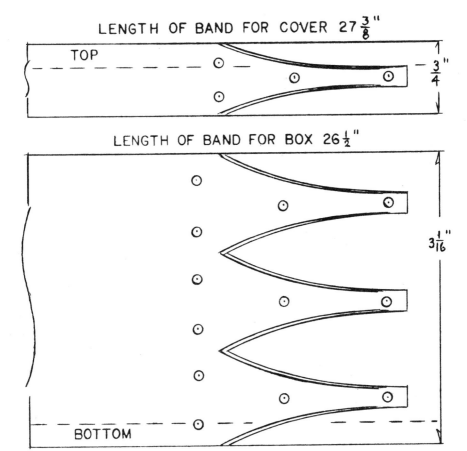

67

CARRIER.

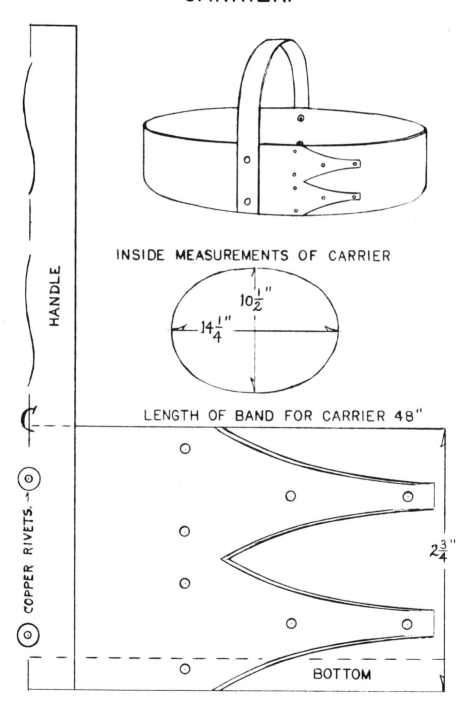

HANDLE

INSIDE MEASUREMENTS OF CARRIER

$10\frac{1}{2}''$

$14\frac{1}{4}''$

LENGTH OF BAND FOR CARRIER 48"

COPPER RIVETS.

$2\frac{3}{4}''$

BOTTOM

CARRIERS.

INSIDE MEAS.
OF CARRIERS
$10\frac{3}{8}$" $\times$ $14\frac{1}{2}$"

HEIGHT TO TOP
OF HANDLE
$9\frac{3}{4}$"

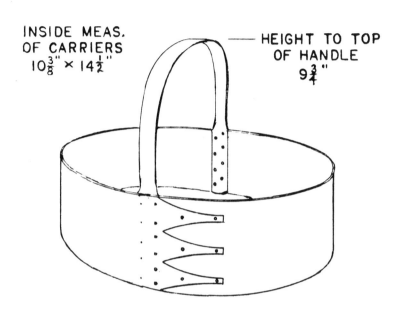

LENGTH OF BAND
FOR CARRIERS
52"

HEIGHT TO TOP
OF HANDLE
$11\frac{1}{4}$"

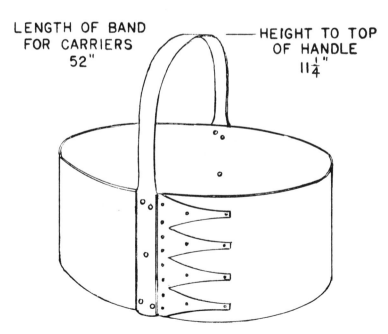

SPITTOON OR "SPIT-BOX"

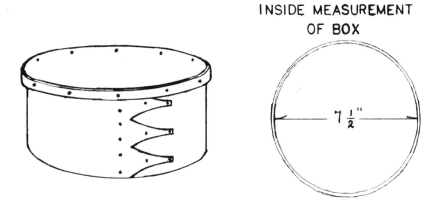

INSIDE MEASUREMENT
OF BOX

$7\frac{1}{2}''$

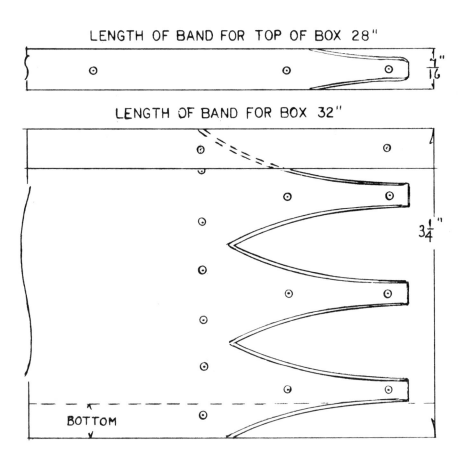

LENGTH OF BAND FOR TOP OF BOX 28"

$\frac{7}{16}''$

LENGTH OF BAND FOR BOX 32"

$3\frac{1}{4}''$

BOTTOM

PINE TRAY 9" × 15"

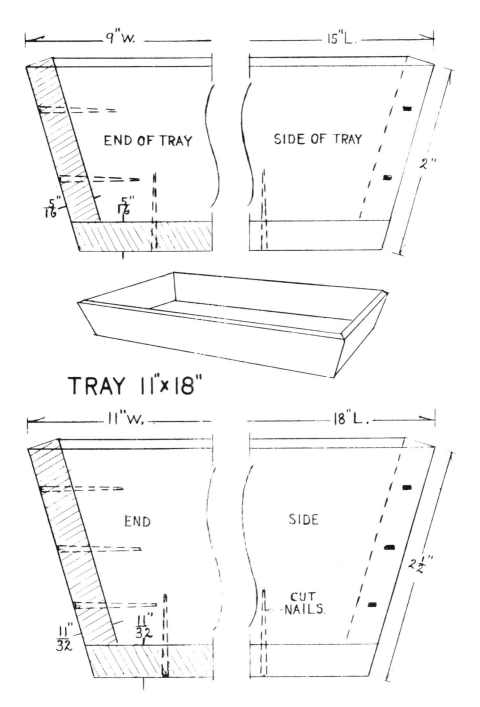

9"w.   15"L.

END OF TRAY   SIDE OF TRAY

2"

$\frac{5}{16}"$ $\frac{5}{16}"$

TRAY 11"× 18"

11"w.   18"L.

END   SIDE

CUT NAILS.

$2\frac{1}{2}"$

$\frac{11}{32}"$ $\frac{11}{32}"$

DINING ROOM TRAY.

SCALE $\frac{1}{4}" = 1"$

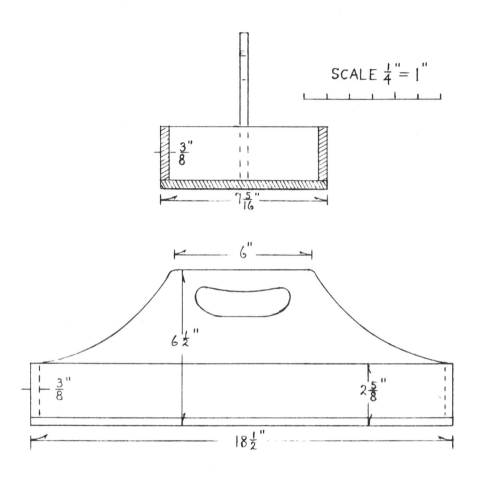

$\frac{3}{8}"$

$7\frac{5}{16}"$

$6"$

$6\frac{1}{2}"$

$\frac{3}{8}"$

$2\frac{5}{8}"$

$18\frac{1}{2}"$

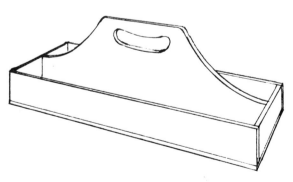

PINE DINING ROOM TRAY.

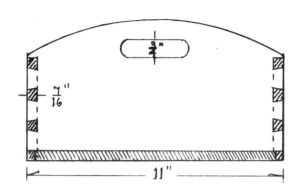

$\frac{3}{4}"$

$\frac{7}{16}"$

11"

SCALE $\frac{1}{4}" = 1"$

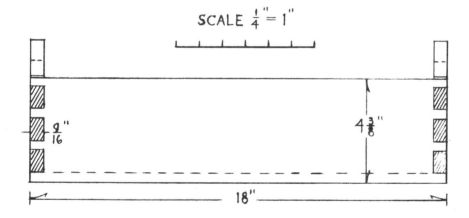

$\frac{9}{16}"$

$4\frac{3}{8}"$

18"

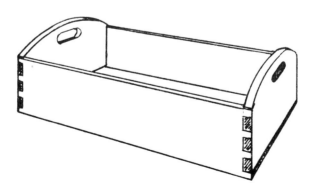

CLAMP-ON
CUSHIONS.

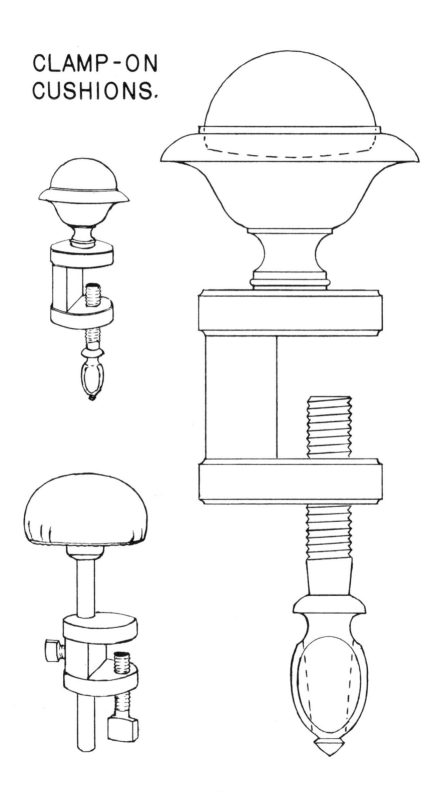

SPOOL HOLDER.

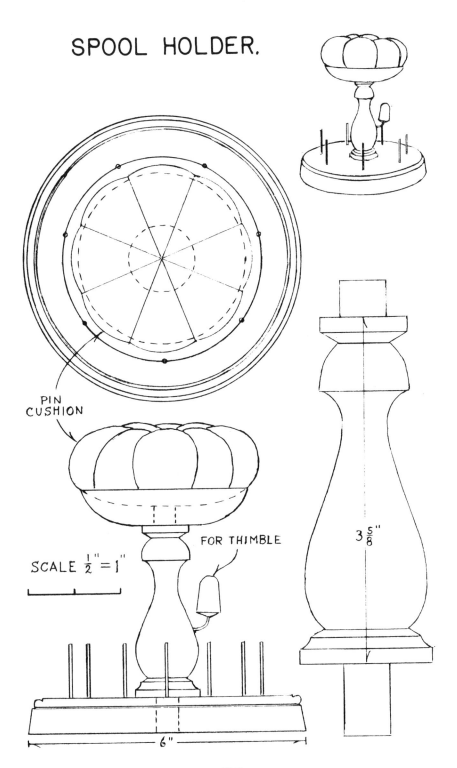

PIN
CUSHION

SCALE $\frac{1}{2}'' = 1''$

FOR THIMBLE

$3\frac{5}{8}''$

6"

DIPPER.

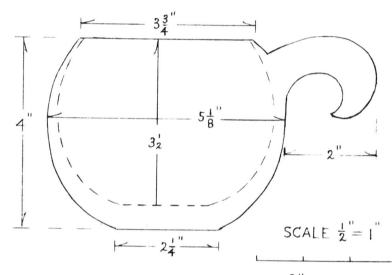

$3\frac{3}{4}''$

$4''$

$5\frac{1}{8}''$

$3\frac{1}{2}'$

$2''$

$2\frac{1}{4}''$

SCALE $\frac{1}{2}'' = 1''$

BERRY BOX.

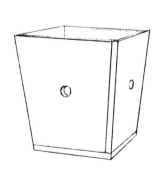

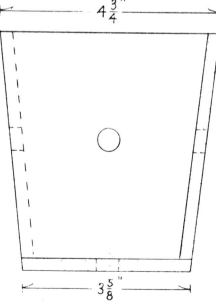

$4\frac{3}{4}''$

$3\frac{5}{8}''$

DIPPER.

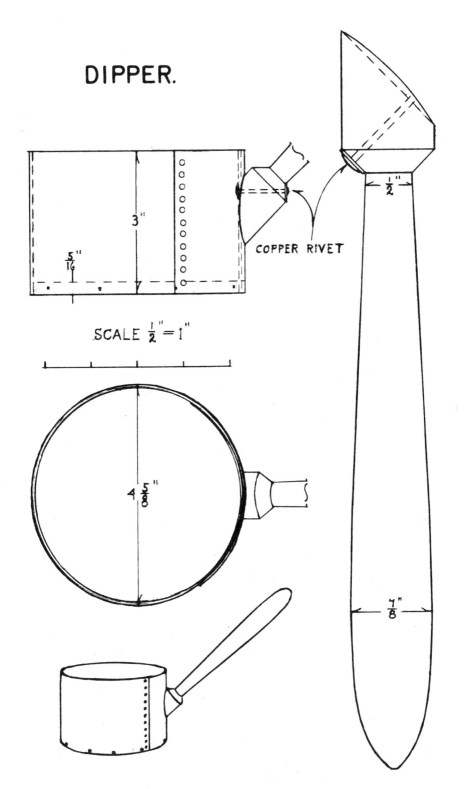

3"

5/16"

COPPER RIVET

1/2"

SCALE 1/2" = 1"

4 5/8"

7/8"

77

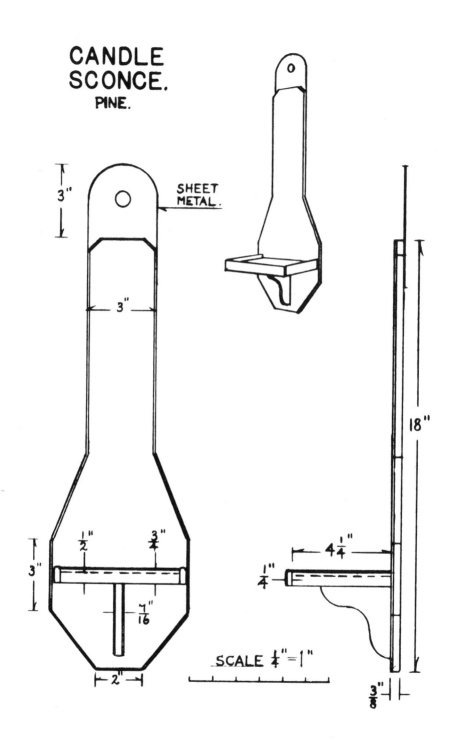

CANDLE
SCONCE.
PINE.

3"

SHEET
METAL.

3"

3"

$\frac{1}{2}$"

$\frac{3}{4}$"

$\frac{7}{16}$"

2"

18"

$4\frac{1}{4}$"

$\frac{1}{4}$"

$\frac{3}{8}$"

SCALE $\frac{1}{4}$"=1"

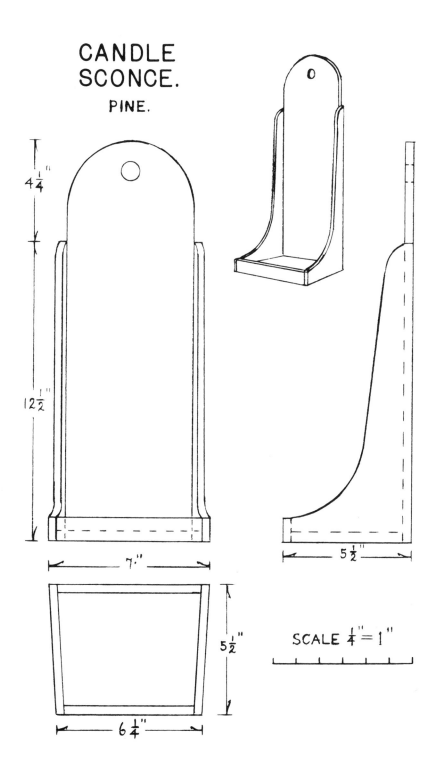

CANDLE
SCONCE.
PINE.

$4\frac{1}{4}$"

$12\frac{1}{2}$"

7"

$5\frac{1}{2}$"

$6\frac{1}{4}$"

$5\frac{1}{2}$"

SCALE $\frac{1}{4}$" = 1"

79.

CANDLESTAND.

CHERRY

SCALE $\frac{1}{4}'' = 1''$

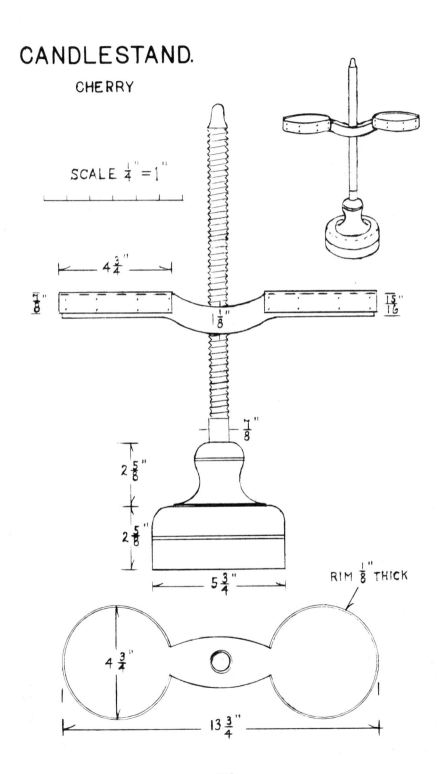

$4\frac{3}{4}''$

$\frac{7}{8}''$

$\frac{1}{8}''$

$\frac{15}{16}''$

$\frac{7}{8}''$

$2\frac{5}{8}''$

$2\frac{5}{8}''$

$5\frac{3}{4}''$

RIM $\frac{1}{8}''$ THICK

$4\frac{3}{4}''$

$13\frac{3}{4}''$

COAT HANGERS.

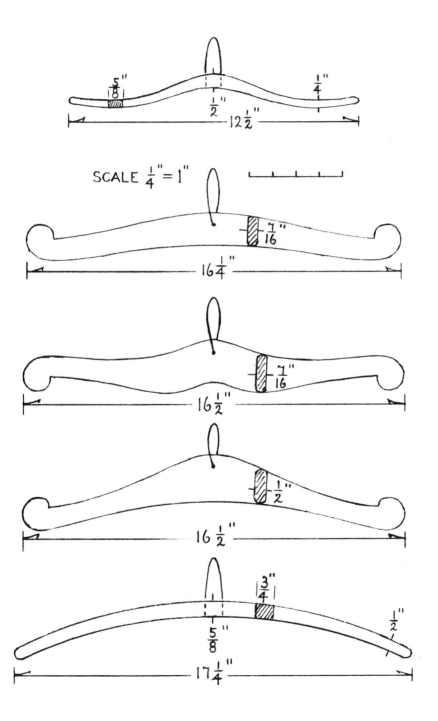

SCALE $\frac{1}{4}$" = 1"

81

INDEX

Asterisks after plate numbers refer to drawings made from pieces in the collection of Dr. and Mrs. Edward D. Andrews.

Ejner Handberg

ABOUT THE AUTHOR

Ejner Handberg is a cabinetmaker of some 50 years experience. He was born in Denmark and came to the United States when he was 17 years old. He learned his craft from oldtime 19th century cabinet makers who insisted upon precision and accuracy.

A number of years ago he first became acquainted with the simplicity and dignity of Shaker furniture as a result of restoring and repairing many original pieces. His reputation in this field grew and the early collectors soon learned of his skill in such restorative work.

At this time, Ejner began to prepare meticulously perfect measured drawings of these original Shaker pieces for the purpose of reproducing them in his own shop one at a time. He made careful notes about the different types of wood used in the originals, and the unique methods of joining. He felt drawn to the basic Shaker designs that were characterized by the abolishment of non-essential ornamentations. He followed, as closely as possible, the reverence that these unusual people had for wood and the purely functional purpose in furniture.

This book, containing 80 of Mr. Handberg's carefully prepared scale drawings, represents much of his life's work. It includes drawings of Shaker chairs, tables, stands, sewing boxes, cupboards, a bed, trestle tables and many other pieces.

The informed amateur worker in wood, as well as the professional cabinetmaker, will find Mr. Handberg's book a valuable addition to the perpetuation of Shaker qualities.